THE PRODIGAL SON

By

Jason "Press" Haynes

ISBN: 0692378782
ISBN-13: 9780692378786
Library of Congress Control Number: 2015904238
Jason Haynes, Brooklyn, New York

Ordering Information:
Quantity sales. Special discounts are available on quantity purchases by corporations, associations, and others. Orders by U.S. trade bookstores and wholesalers also welcomed.
For details, questions, and purchases, please see contact information below.
Email: theprodigalson81@gmail.com

Printed in the United States of America.

The loss of my mother at a very young age was tough on all sides. My father's love was assertive, confident, militant, protective, unemotional yet still present. Bred off street survival and instincts, he embraced fatherhood the only way he knew best...his way. Even though we never saw eye to eye, his ability to handle adversity offensively, to attack life with persistence and discipline was second to none. Comparatively different to my emotional, artistic, and spontaneous personality that needed a nurturing counterpart to him. It seemed the only thing we had in common was the propensity to argue.

Through the hardships of homelessness, the prison system, bouts with depression and lethargy...I called upon a God who steered me through my darkest hours. When I had no answers left, He was right on time. This book serves as a return to an eternal Father's grace and a counsel to the downtrodden. For those who seek inspiration through the storms, may the shelter of these words find you...enjoy.

In Loving Memory

Of

Patricia Keith

Table of Contents

Prologue

Home, Sweet, Home

From the tightly sewn costumes in carnivals replayed
To the jovial sounds of the steel drum we played.
We watched the young and old have their problems
whisked away by the melodic strums of Calypso.
From the women, whose hips brought visual illusions.
Gyrating as if it were a separate entity
from the rest of the body.
To the drinks I knew I couldn't touch
when mixed with the right amount of rum,
like Ponche-de-Crème.
Trinidad, an island of celebrations.
We would drink a tree bark-based beverage called Mauby,
Along with the enjoyment
of a Christmas pastime favorite…Sorrel.
Roti, bake & saltfish, doubles, crab & calaloo.

We would eat heartily.
Sweet, sweet, T&T…

I remember in the early dawn at eight or nine years old,
entrusted at 5am to travel alone to school.
A procession of taxis on the main road
became daily escorts.
On the lookout for customers moving cautiously
Like a presidential motorcade during a parade.
Colorful brick houses with aluminum roofing,
illuminating the landscape from the sun's rays.
The weary eyes of the homeless,
Surveying their landscape for answers
To an equation that brought more questions.
The economy was tough; jobs were scarce.
We had two channels on television,
And a loaf of bread was six dollars.
My grandmother's shower was located outside.
Most days we had no hot water,

And a bucket caught the rain on torrential nights
as it leaked relentlessly through a porous roof.
Yet the fun days were enjoyed at the Savanna.
I remember going with my father to most places,
Even to the horse racing tracks
where a son's lucky picks enabled his habit.
Kids would play soccer barefoot all day
on those grassy fields;
our shoes used as goalposts.
Neither time nor bills mattered back then.
Sweet, sweet T&T…

The best of times was upon my return.
Older now, I remember the spectacular red sightings
of the Scarlet Ibis in the Caroni Swamp.
I remember being off the north eastern tip
Where on a clear day you can see the island of Tobago,
And hear the raucous sounds of the Cocrico at dusk.
Resting on a hammock

tied between two coconut palm trees.

With warm weather all year round

mixed in with a tropical storm or two.

I watched the pristine view of blue and green waters,

And felt its cool ocean breeze.

I heard the sounds of waves gently kissing the rocks

And then I knew…

This country was more than just memories

My last sight was of a snail

steadily climbing a hibiscus flower leaf.

Then my eyes closed…

Peaceful thoughts of a return home,

to familiar grounds where a mother was buried.

She was closer to me now.

It was the best sleep I ever had.

Home, sweet, home.

The story goes that on her deathbed she asked my father

to promise never to leave her son with anyone else.

And he never did.

I saw "Pops" cry twice in my life.

Only one needed to be the toughest.

The day her eyes closed for a final time.

Never again had I seen and felt

so much pain in a single tear.

But on her passing day and beyond,

His mourning turned to anger.

Things would never be the same again…

I. The American Dream

Mice & Men

Different apartments had various acoustics.

The mesh of ambiance and carpeting determined

how successful those wintry nights would go.

The dips in temperature seemed to bring in all

the rodents from the back dumpsters

of this New York snow,

to hibernate & feast on their survival instincts.

If there was food to be eaten;

if a scent filled the midnight air...

…they would know.

It was only year one in America.

Brooklyn to be exact.

No beds available but we made due.

Sheets unceremoniously laid out gently on the carpet

as if dead bodies were silently respected,

while the stench grew...smelled like a mouse.

Two senses heightened

as these grey grizzly mini-bears were always heard,

but rarely seen in the still of the night.

And this fright prevents the luxury of sleep as I wait...

Just maybe the poisons, the sticky & cheese traps

will do its job and lure this smart creature into his fate.

The soap opera of the late hour.

Toss & turn o' young & restless soul,

dwelling under the safety of thick comforters

to shelter the warmth from the cold...

Dreams were hard to conceptualize back then.

The sum of all fears,

the cacophony of howls from canines,

shrieks from felines outside,

matching the faint falsettos of famine inside,

critters yearning to feast on crumbs.

It was as if these rodents

were staging this mental musical in my light slumber.

But this dark symphony drifted,

as thoughts shifted...to the dawn.

Light breaks as the half-opened window sill

ushers in its fresh breeze.

"the early bird catcheth the worm".[1]

But "blessed is that second mouse,

For he shall inherit the cheese".[2]

However, on this day, when opportunity knocks,

it's the stench of complacency that can unlock

Bolstered doors with skeleton keys.

And there you shall find him...

caught between wood & metal.

Darkness ruled the night

yet patience was my awakened eye,

in this realm of mice and men and mangled things.

But in my world, in the kingdom of the blind,

The one eyed man is indeed king.[3]

Store run

My identity was found on New York Avenue.

We moved up and down this familiar road.

Each corner lived, had its own story;

the grim and the glory.

I remember of one I deemed the cemetery.

The literal & figurative dually applied here.

A few blocks away…the "official" bodies laid.

Within that distance dues where paid.

Only two lights brightened their radius.

A lamp post on dying legs drained of its nightly duties

watching the day's events.

The other was The Bodega…

This corner store was the jack of all trades.

Supplying household products & habits,

Housing false hopes and increasing debt.

Enablers of the neighborhood,

As long as currency was met.

Its walls harbored many vices inside and out.

We found its purpose.

Dice chipped against stone,

Ceelo was the favorite of the grown.

New English was spoken through 'Olde English'

As 40 oz. bottles spilled on drenched bricks

to the backdrop of excited & loud tones.

But more commonly, during the nights activities,

Semen usually found its home.

True to his culture,

my father labored through many jobs,

sacrificed through long hours.

Yet one of the many duties of the apartment

included the storerun.

Stepping outside after ten o' clock

was always an adventure.

The night had its power.

But you embrace it, face it…never cower.

The walk included the occasional "what's good lil man?"

You give respect and move on in the darkness.

…That lamp post felt so far away…

As his siblings flickered.

Futile attempts to stay awake.

They would finally rest…

Upon entrance of most corner stores,

there were always three.

One at the door, another at the counter

And the last, somewhere in the back.

Rarely was the latter seen,

But when you saw him,

he always saw you first

as he anxiously checked inventory.

No one really knew their names or ethnicity.

Usually called "Habib" or "Papi" by frequent customers.

Each store run had hopeful gamblers holding up the line,

playing their winning tickets.

All I cared about was making sure this line was short,

In and out like a robbery.

But on this night,

This gambler held seven tickets to be checked.

The excitement from the dice game grew,

"Habib" from the door,

runs to the counter to assist the line.

Finally taken care of,

Yet the outside commotion could not be ignored.

"Habib" from inventory rushes out,

Annoyed with a well-worn wooden Louisville slugger.

He exits store and vehemently says,

"Take it down the block before I call the cops!"

Back then law enforcement rarely came
For the trivial nuances of the hood.
Their hands rather filled with sugary substances
Than pens and paperwork.

With two bags of bread, milk and other things…I left.
Now the cautionary stroll turned into a brisk walk
As voices rose behind me,
I knew that this was no ordinary argument.
Seconds later, these three or four gamblers of the night
Rounded corners out of sight.
Then it was heard…
Pop. Pop. Pop!
Bloodcurdling screams of fear
Mixed with agony and desperation.
Dogs barked in response.
Apartment lights turned on.
It happened so quickly…

No time to look back like Lot's wife.

The code was to never stick around

For the streets in days ahead will mumble its crimes.

Usually the curious ended up

in the wrong places and at the wrong times.

Never did I look back

until safety was the dominant environment.

Home sweet home.

The distant sounds of EMS;

the red sirens of the law

and the twinkles of the midnight sun

illuminate the pimples of a beautiful continence.

The forecast of more to come.

Oh how the face of a hood can change

on a simple store run.

Survival of the Fittest

Back in the 90s,

Baggy pants, fresh Jordans, Hilfiger, Coogi,

Fubu, Nautica, Rocawear, Polo ran the yard.

Anything found fraudulent subjected you to the school diss.

Name brands determined your status

in the hierarchy of coolness.

From the West Indies hot December sun to a cool mist.

In pursuit of the American dream,

Ignorance gave way to rules missed.

But the culture was difficult to comprehend.

So I wrote my goals on paper and made a fool's list.

Placed in the hood,

the fingers of book and commonsense required teamwork.

So I formed a cruel fist.

Façades to cliques

Was like a shoehorn to a newly worn heel…
…simple tools used to fit in.
The price of comfort always on the outward appearance,
never on the feel.
The attention to detail was in defense
against the celebration of the worthless.
Instead of books never in bags to transport things,
Crazy glue used on knots just to protect Jansport strings.
On the playgrounds, to be in Jordan's air was likely.
But as MJ got paid, my pops made a career
In multiple jobs spending shares of checks,
just so that I can wear a pair of his Nikes.
Bullies played their part,
forcing many to man up nightly.
But the mind and body can only form its true posture,
when the heart can stand uprightly.

Fights, stickups, and jumpings lurked the streets.
Death in broad daylight.

Other outcomes in darkened corners.
Veiling shades of plundered ones.
The dangerous spoke in friendly tones
With blades under tongues.
Shoes strung on wires above;
Yellow tape swung around poles
cordoning off scenes below.
Chalk outlining untold stories.
Young businessmen on corners
applying their classroom subjects daily.
Trigonometry, Chemistry and Marketing.
They understood the functions of angles,
recognizing social cues and signals in the laws of *Sines*
when stories went on *Tangents*.
Grams and ounces priced methodically
Elements quantified on tables periodically.
Word of mouth marketing,
Direct selling to the consumer.

Birthed in these streets of survival for most
is where entrepreneurial skills grew.
The art of the hustle perfected
as the pressure mounts when those bills due.
When everything goes wrong;
The only thing the fruits of your labor can show is mildew.
When your back is up against the walls,
never underestimate the power of your resolve.
Darwin's instincts honed
for these under-resourced environments
where hesitation and doubt kills you.
But I don't care who's the strongest,
the fastest or the smartest.
Put me in any arena with the most talented
because they don't know what I've been through.
And let me show them that in the end,
I can still out-will you.

II. Broken Home

Solitude

Supposedly, I should've had a big sister.

Never meant to be.

But sent to me was the lonely mile.

The solitude of an only child.

The assumption between my father and I was

The son always 'spoiled' with love and affection,

Immigrants attempting to catch

the wave of the American Dream on its ascension.

But the reality was filled with tension.

We landed fresh off the boat,

Too broke to pay attention.

He was both mother and father.

Working three jobs to make ends meet

It became his cross to bear.

So his feelings became a martyr.

For starters, a sibling of thirteen,

middle name Michael.

Poverty only enlightened his struggle

for a mother's affection.

Hence, only breeding another vicious cycle.

Most days I wished for a sibling to be my sponge,

to help absorb the mental blows.

But the hood was merciless.

Unforgiving in its dealings;

always a brush with fate.

The House always won,

Survival became a cerebral weight.

The gamble was uncertain.

Even when the mind was in a royal flush state.

Yet as a child in my privacy,

I was able to use whatever was around to create.

To shape, mold, remake objects and characters.

The mind of a potter's hands

Yearning for his approval

Precise notes of a blemished personality were listed.

Now as I got older, all I wanted to do

Was to pretend he never existed.

Sergeant

For some all it took was a look.

That look which says "just try me child".

For other less fortunate West Indians,

there was no warning.

Born in a system of corporal punishment.

Wisdom of the rod cracked in venues

where any elder statesman could walk up

smack the God back in you.

In our halls of higher learning,

bamboo sticks were delicately wrapped in electrical tape.

Varying colors for different educational levels

and personal tastes piquant to the mind.

Yellow, teal, lavender, white, brown, black.

Teacher's pets willing to do their master's bidding.

The red pet was reserved for the principal.

Stronger, tightly wound;

less likely to break upon the buttocks of his victims.
Hands extended for the less egregious.

The obedient survived,
with their correct answers and perfect scores.
For others, two or three pairs of underwear
worn inconspicuously before the entrance of those doors.
Many cried, pleading cases of tears
that landed on the runway of deaf ears.
Few never moved nor uttered a sound...

Home was just as rigid.
The warnings were felt before the beatings.
"If yuh nuh gon hear, yuh gon feel!"
And "yuh monkey gland raising!"
If your punishment was ever corporal,
then you've met the Sergeant.
If you've ever had to pick out the tools

for your own whipping...

Switches, belts, cords, wood, paddles,

You've met the sergeant.

If you've ever had to run in the same spot

Because the pain wouldn't let you move,

You've met the sergeant.

If the only way you could sleep

was on your sides or stomach,

You've met the sergeant.

The invisible markings of discipline.

Seventeenth century philosopher John Locke believed that

"children who have been the most chastised

seldom make the best men".[4]

But he believed in subjecting kids

to cold temperatures and wet shoes.

Yet my grandmother's favorite husbands

were Solomon and King James.

As the belt would sing in midswing...she would say,

"Foolishness is bound in the heart of a child;

but the rod of correction shall drive it far from him."[5]

It sung again...

“Spare the rod, spoil the child”[6]

(Even though that wasn’t from the Bible).

It sung louder…

"The rod and reproof give wisdom:

But a child left to himself bringeth his mother to shame."[7]

But maybe the shame is in attempting not to understand

The inner workings of a child's mind.

Engagement which allows personalities to shine.

Let the discipline of the rod

never override the discipline of your time.

III. Stagnancy

Stuck

What train? This train going to nowhere...
Yes, my destination is in the future,
but I was stuck here, in the present.

As I sat there,
these passengers were strangers
yet some became subconscious allies
against death's mercenary...Time.
The grumblings of him, the one who did not sit still,
but looked through the train's glass for answers,
but all he received were the loud sounds of metal & sparks.
As time showed her speed, the stops went by;

he rejoices...

Ever so slightly with a grin

that resembles a joker playing poker,

hiding his winning hand, yet displaying all of his answers.

That grin filled with the smirk of a conquering king.

But he has met a worthy opponent.

An ardent adversary,

who has wiped historical grins off the jolliest of giants,

outflanked and subdued the most powerful of rulers.

A formidable foe whose moves

could be as loud as the timpani drum

amongst his peers in this symphony

of New York City jeers.

Because today he moves

as subtly as the Caribbean South wind.

Creeping ever so silently upon his prey,

unawares, in a hammock of comfort and consistency...

...when the train stops.

Time…

this double agent of the gods who threads needles

between joy and misery,

has overcome his foe.

As the passenger who once shown

the smiles of a thousand kings,

shakes a bowed head in disappointment.

The sullen countenance of defeat as he realizes

that time will always win.

And the only way we can slow time down,

is if we can somehow slow ourselves...

He is late for a meeting,

Intently engaged in a pressure filled dichotomy…

Willing his train to speed up

As his eyes try to thrust the brakes on the clock's tick.

She holds her child with the infinite questions for

tomorrow.

Blank stares through her window

past the shrieks and sparks of metal.

In search for assistance from a 25th hour

between work, school, motherhood and sleep.

I shall take this next breath deeply and appreciate this ride,

Positioned at a standstill between two stops...

...going nowhere.

If Only Dreams Had Wings

If only these dreams had wings.

Could you transcend the moments like

"You ain't gonna be nothing"

"You Kermit da frog, pencil looking, longneck bastard".

"You're too fat" or "You're too slow".

People shoot verbal bullets that can penetrate

The vests of the very best,

Plunging some off mental cliffs.

I guess that's why I spit for all the broken hearts

Left with embedded track marks

still desperate for an emotional lift.

I spit for her deflated dreams punched by hidden myths,

Because her body could only equate her perception of love

By how well she can absorb a fist.

I spit for all the section eight campers,

the group homers and food stampers.

Because I remember the days when I had less than most,
But I still knew how to use an aluminum foil and an iron
to make some great damn toast.

I spit for all those concrete nomads in the cold,
Who knows how to comfortably tuck their blankets
under their sides and toes,
Just to cushion their hips and sleep off their woes.
I spit for all those artistic souls
Behind bars and locks,
in Genpops rocking jumpers & flops,
Who can creatively suspend time with pushups and a pad,
Or by carefully chiseling minds,
Carving books into chess pieces and glocks.
Yet if only these dreams had wings,
Could I nest in homes
where nightly cries from life's miserable memories
Can finally reach the precipice of the tipping point

in their mental cellblocks.

But here behind these prisons and walls,

You and I are free.

Where I will condense hours to minutes;

I will not break,

nor will I follow the flock.

But in the end I will use my mind and pen

to bend this time to my own clock.

If only these dreams had wings.

Many times I felt stuck on my constellation's 13th floor,

Like the high-jinx or bad luck of life's trials

Just went amuck somewhere within heaven's shroud.

Yet if only these dreams had wings,

Could I fall from thirteen

But still land on that 9th cloud.

Could I look down from above

and glide through hoods

Where fixed eyes took lives

And loose tongues met young guns,

But I can look back and show kids

That being in control of a weapon can win battles,

But knowing who you are and what you stand for as men.

To control one's emotions

is where those true wars are won.

I bring these words in a way

that can inspire you to be the next Claude Mckay,

Counte Cullen poetic thriller

of this day.

So before you start swinging a gun thinking you're a killer,

Pick up a book so I can teach you about a real guerilla

named Che.

If only these dreams had wings

Could I stretch my arms into heaven

And wrap these numb limbs

around my mother in my hardest of adversities.

So that I will always endure and be comforted in knowing

That she has always been smiling,

watching down over me since nursery.

Now what was once seen as a mountain

was only a molehill,

And those goose bumps only came from

The truth I spat making bodies quiver.

Now if only my dreams had wings,

Could I flap out cool thoughts

That would make even a wind draft shiver.

Or how about those thoughts that expresses

Frustration when puddles become rivers.

And with each passing day,

All that life can express to you in return

Is some tattered down cliché.

"Son, sometimes when it rains, it pours"[8]

But if my way was somehow lost,

Could I circle heaven's realm

until I found those pearly doors.

Because narrow is my road

And that's where I saw my limelight shining.

So if only my dreams had wings,

Could I sift through those grey clouds

And still find that silver lining.

If only these dreams had wings,

And any other parts needed to get my craft going.

I would be in my mind's eye

Showing kids how to draft crafts in thin air while honing

Ideas from thoughts flowing,

Knowing that when their dreams have wings,

They can brainstorm late at thirteen minutes to eight

And still assemble more aircrafts than Boeing.

And in case it was missed in the beginning why I spit.

I spit for all the charismatic dreamers

Who hope and hustle no matter what their situation entails,
against all cynics and pragmatics.
Hold on.
I'm not Irving or Jordan
But I can still dribble these words
with this Mike and still do Magic.
Hold on.
For I will be your linguistic inhaler
Filled with verbal albuterol,
Pumping this lyrical lexicon through your lungs
when your life feels asthmatic.

So let these dreams have wings,
because I'm flying against the wind…
Resistance is just a test to me.
I developed some ideas
And the nay-sayers tried to get the best of me.
But their moral insecurities will not affect my destiny.

Bite into this Lifesaver and digest,

Behind every sweet truth is clarity.

Never be distracted by the flavor of the month

…my Grandmother would always say…

Behind every sweet tooth is a cavity.

So focus, stretch your imagination

And let your headspace defy gravity.

Let your dreams defy all reason

So that in reality you are encouraged

in and out of season.

IV. Obstacle Course

The Air Smelled Different.

Maybe it was the pungent cries of sweat glands.

Their scents yearning to be released into the world.

Maybe it was the heat fueling the unwashed feet

and hygiene of reality.

The signs of inmates refusing to become adjusted to it.

Maybe it was the smell of commissary.

Brown paper bags filled

with soap, deodorant, cookies and crackers.

Bread and peanut butter were the luxury items

Used to barter deals like cleanup duty and phone time.

The signs of a few, already adjusted to this life...

Maybe it was the air of ingenuity.

A hot water bucket filled with packets of ramen noodles.

Pillows used to trap the steam and harness its spices.
Portions dispersed evenly.
This goulash became a small social event of the night.
Too many people attracted unwanted attention.
The aroma disguised other herbs
hidden from guards.

Maybe it was the lingering air of fear.
The intense stares from real eyes doing bids in years,
able to distinguish the cubs from the bears.
Maybe it was the atmosphere of the unknown.
Phone calls were precious conversations
That hid tears and groans.
Lawyers and loved-ones supplied hope on loans.
Moments truncated in minutes.
But waiting your turn had its limits.
Joy, pain, passion, disappointment, and anger;
Optimism at its best, frustration at its worst.
Guards with an axe to grind,

relishing in this modicum of power and control.

All stuffed in the balloon of patience,

Growing until it bursts…

Egos, affiliations, and 72” industrial sized fans

recirculating humid air back through the dormitories.

All contributing to its roles as disruptors of peace.

Isolations and lockdowns, slashings and black eyes;

stimulus for social control between corruptors and beasts.

Maybe it was the breeze of temptation.

Planes loudly establishing their route

over the majestic Manhattan skyline.

The clang of metal…

From the closings of cellblocks

To the jingling of keys

Dangling off a guard’s hip like a bunch of grapes.

Ready to be plucked by hungry eyes

awaiting an opportunity.

Maybe it was the draft of change.
Newbies, transfers and veterans
Exchanged through the system
until friends soon became estranged.
Mattresses removed or rearranged
To cushion the powers of time,
Able to make the soundest mind deranged.

Or maybe it was that crisp morning chill
when fates are determined.
While in transport, the eerie chill of nerves
mingled with the weather of destiny.
Yet in the holding cells we prayed,
Awaiting a final meeting with a judge I had no faith in.
$800 bond given for threats never uttered.
Menacing charges falsely trumped up by a father,
Who brilliantly ignored due process with a clever ploy.
May his conscience find peace,
until seen on judgment day with his only boy.

Maybe it was the fragrance of God
Covering pores and glands;
Blowing the winds of adversity
out those courtroom doors with His opened hands.
Either way…

The air smelled different.

I stood outside with my head to the skies.
Dampened clothes from the drizzle of rain,
smelling the air of freedom with closed eyes.
Though I can walk where I choose again,
This air didn't fill my physical state.
I left everything at Rikers Island.
No belt to support filthy jeans.
My favorite New York Yankees hat
to cover an unshaven head was left.
No deodorant or cologne
to mask the stench through a stained shirt.

No laces to tie worn shoes.

No money for a cab.

No job to return to.

No place to call home.

But none of that mattered.

Because in the deep recesses of the mind

where no jail cell or misfortune can touch;

but where all worries are laid on mattresses of hope

and all doubts are covered with blankets of faith…

…you can still find the comforts of home.

Blindspot

He was my blind spot.

Loyalty and denial were my eyes,

So I couldn't see his vehicle too busy looking at the skies,

But I should have seen the sign stops.

I couldn't get a feel for the steering,

Because a termite was eating my wheels,

Tires tearing and I was fearing losing my pops,

So like food stamps,

I gave him free meals to my mental steel,

But the protein in the veal

exposed lies of a character that wasn't real.

I needed a shield

But he chewed away at that confidence

until my grind stopped.

In the end, he was sitting there

with a full stomach of control

watching my mind rot.

But complacency can only control

the hours of the day that you give it,

So I've learned to never fit it in my timeslot.

I crafted these bars in my rhyme shop,

Then laid them away from the shade,

Under the raid of the heat

But under the cross of the Son they stayed,

That's what made these lines hot.

I tried to drive straight.

My opportunity was at five,

But I tried to defy fate.

To survive was a trait,

I never cut corners

But my mind was never in a nine to five state.

Preparation was never early.

So now I'm moving fast to win it,

But all it takes is that one left turn

in that blind spot last minute.

Bow! I'm alive, wait.

The lesson, if your aim is to always just be on time,

Your blessings will always arrive late.

We all have a blind spot.

Each eye has a small area of the retina

Where there are no visual receivers.

Leaving a tiny gap; nothing can be seen.

The brain "fills in" that gap from what it interprets

from the other eye.

So I tested it.

I drew a dot and a cross 6-8in apart on a sheet of paper.

Covered my right eye

and focused on the cross with my right.

I allowed my peripheral vision to see the dot on the left.

Then slowly brought the paper towards my face.

While my focus was still on the cross,

I noticed the dot disappeared as I drew closer.[9]

A physiological gun for a family member

to psychologically get in your holster.

You see this whole country was built on blind spots.

From the ropes we've hung from.

To the marches in Selma,

burned churches and pulpits we sung from.

The cotton fields picked and harvested.

The stones of the capitol building,

Roads paved and a white house dome

built by those 400 slaves.

But you can find them under the waves of the Atlantic.

They roam like forgotten ghosts of the slave trade,

the bones of our graves.

Forgotten sins…

Like my father,

When no light hits the retina of our prejudices,

You find the hearts of the dim.

We can adjust our mirrors to blind spots.

But if our eyes are windows to the soul,

Then we are just pupils to paltry perceptions.

Maybe we just need to adjust our lens,

Meager minds manipulated by myopic men.

Lipstick on a Pig

Its been weeks removed from choosing enjoyment.
I packed emotional luggage in my Jansport
That ended up on transport to the island.
Cruising dormant, the pursuit of happiness
weighed down by years of just scraping by.
Now I'm bruising in torment.

Six weeks removed from losing employment.
Five weeks removed from sleeping in motels to floors
to the backseat of cars, which was fine.
Compared to resting on cold metal beds
Looking through windows hinged by bars that shine
off moonlit nights, decorated by barbed wires and time.
Eyeing the constellation just trying to figure out
which star was mine.

Four weeks removed from being face to face
with the man who put me there.
No joy in view
when you have to be escorted by the boys in blue.
You would think I had a slew of felonies.
But it was a mental crew of enemies
harboring a few jealousies.
There was always some new hypocritical act
illuminating his care.
Maybe because the brew of resentment
was too much to bear.
Three weeks removed from when doubt found powers,
minutes became hours,
so those gates of trust soon became towers.
The stench was just as high,
so those public restrooms soon became showers.
And in my hunger, I saw the hospitality of one,
so her food soon became ours.

I'm grateful for those blessings both small and big.

Even when the muggy air alone,

can test your deodorant and cologne,

covering up flaws like lipstick on a pig.

Today I look back on the day I saw him.

Physically I saw the man who put me there.

His lipstick was lies and manipulation

smudging the face of trust,

Disgust leaving the distaste

of a ton of makeup,

the byproduct of disgrace and lust

melted and dried under heat leaving traces of crust.

But mentally I saw the sinister shoes

of pride's soles on our necks.

It was his pride of control and mine to not walk away.

And in that mirrored moment,

I saw my father's reflection…

…I saw myself...

Two peas in a pod;

stubborn until the end.

Imprisoned through life by a father’s love

That preached standing up for one’s self.

Only to be placed in prison by him,

The day I finally did.

Two weeks removed from a job.

Today, I had to let him go

wishing him the best in all his endeavors.

Standing in front of a check cashing store

with teardrops soiling my signature on an old friend.

Content with the possibility

that I may never see my father again.

The Gamblers

They came in different amounts

Singles, deuces, fives, tens & twenties.

These 4x6 paper vacuums with no sockets,

The dirt devil demons of free will

Sucking every bill from my pockets.

Some days they controlled your fate,

Cured altered states…

These paper Gypsies and Shamans.

Other times they controlled what you ate,

Some days it would be steak

On others it would be Ramen.

Some days my accomplice and I would truly wait,

Slithering thru the grass of lottery busts like two snakes…

Other days we'd be too late.

Golden tickets to nowhere.

But with no care and reckless abandonment we played.

Afraid of only God and probability.

Little did we understand the mathematical impossibilities

given to impoverished areas.

Yet contagious is the scratch off once it touches the hand.

Passed on, blown to the next man

Like Malaria with a fan.

Causing hysteria in the air,

Whether a twenty is flipped into a hundred

Or a deuce is flipped into a five.

Whether you have or have not,

Arrogant or shy,

You can lose two hundred easily in the blink of an eye.

And now you find yourself attempting to break even,

just trying to survive.

Lives monopolized by a mirage of lies.

Thirsty are we in this desert

of high unemployment frictions.

Desperate for some relief,

yet the only cactus we receive

Arrives in the form of more liquor stores

With lottery doors

Open to feed our addictions.

Or just maybe the powers that be in this world,

the beast who serves our cravings.

Understands that our culture

Is always quick to spend,

ready to splurge

But does the least saving.

Yet all we've felt

were those rocks thrown from the ramblers,

The peanut gallery of vast noises.

But whom are the real gamblers,

Sleeping soundly in glass houses.

America holds 2 million inmates

in state, federal, and private prisons.

We've locked up more folks than any other country.

We hold 25% of the world's prison population,

But only 5% of the world's people.[10]

That's half a million more

With a population five times less than China.

Because the prison industry is big business.

Wealthy tycoons and politicians alike,

Eating from enormous plates.

States selling off their prison blocks to eager investors,

As long as they maintain their incarceration rates.

No worries about unemployment benefits,

Punctuality, strikes or vacations.

The only trip you can take is to isolation,

If you don't appreciate the $.25/hour pay at your station.

We produce their military gears

and dress our soldiers well for the cause

Off the sweat stained backs of Hispanics and Blacks.

Send them off for their tours

To stay in countries unwanted for so long,

They soon become forgotten wars.

Bring them back in coffins & crutches

from defending our shores.

Many roam dead end streets

Panhandling just to make ends meet.

Others supplied with lifetime dosages of PTSD.

The rewards for their bravery.

Yet prisons will always serve a need

For wall street to stock their prison portfolios

with hypocrisy and greed.

Big business living in an ecosystem of modern day slavery.

So who are the true gamblers??

Is it the decadent dreams of the destitute,

simply destined into more debt??

Or is it the hidden poker countenances

of corporate capitalists

Doubling down on sure bets?

Snapping out of it, I passed by a convenience store.

Long lines of the optimistic;

hope in numbers.

Golden tickets to nowhere.

The Hate

I love it when they talk about you.

Doubt you.

They criticize the strides

in your step because they see from the sides

a certain walk about you.

They whisper, as if you hid crimes or did time.

Their talk cast judgments on a body of work

that couldn't see its prime,

cut off by the mouths of yellow tape,

drawing lines of chalk round you.

The ones closest to you can do the most surprising things

that would astound you.

Some view themselves as friends

so watch who's around you.

They see your plane about to lift off,

they try to ground you.

Yet the minute you hit your destination,

they try to surround you.

Then ask them how they knew you,

they'd swear they found you.

For some the majority rules their positions.

Others have none.

Ask them to speak their minds and they become politicians.

Some disappear for years then reappear like apparitions.

Ghosts subtracted from the dream,

became a division to the vision.

Then there are the clever ones

who suffer from selfish ambitions.

They genuinely wish you the best in whatever you do…

until you become their competition.

They say great minds think alike,

but great minds think for themselves.

So dust my gifts off those shelves.

No catch, no exceptions,

no fine print, no clause, no elves.

But alone I was taught

as I let my tone unwrap presents thru your ears

into the homes of your thoughts.

So that when my pen combs thru tough hair,

I can pick your brain n roam thru neural zones

with these poems that I brought.

So remember the few

who invested their hearts in the mental drain

while others threw pennies in your fountains.

But in all your doubting,

mustard seeds can only truly be sown

in the soil of your souls to move those mountains.

So I'm counting these blessings,

because no matter the dirt thrown,

your gifts were never meant to be buried,

but always sent to be grown.

V. Love & Lust

Sweat

Can I be your sweat?

Beautiful, brown skin...

This amalgamation of your kinetic and heat laws.

But it's from the center of your erotic core

that opens doors to those erogenous floors,

where I can drift down and explore

where gravity can take me some more.

Where I can saturate your every body's desires

and permeate its pores.

Let me tingle your spine while I rekindle your mind

with a sense of touch so good,

your body can say "no sex",

but watch me work that cerebellum like a bow flex

till both get sore.

Yea, I want to be your sweat...
Where I can take this journey slow
and moisten every crevice from head to toe.
because I am the manifestation of your hard day's work,
so no matter what your ailments are,
I want to be your remedy.
Lyrically stimulate your nerve endings
until my tongue can numb all of your extremities.
Then let my fingers
physically tune your moans to the perfect pitch,
so that my brass can play the right melodies.
Picture me, this salt/ water mixture
exploring every magnificent contour of your terrain.
Picture me traversing every seductive curve,
detailing every nook and cranny,
traveling through every hill and valley

of your perfect frame.

Picture me being the byproduct

of what your man can never be.

Picture me so that by the time I'm done with you,

you can picture him being a memory.

But let me replace your tears,

With shoes of rain to dance down your cheeks

And caress your lips.

I want to synchronize my moves to those melodic hips.

Following your lead while the classics soothingly play.

We can role-play to "a house is not a home" or I can be

"easy like Sunday morning".

We can feel brand new with The Stylistics

or we can even jazz this thing up

with some freestyles of Miles…Whatever.

You can be gay for your Marvin,

and I'll be a little Pip for my Gladys,
Just so long as I can face the sweet embrace of your smiles.

Yea, I want to linger in between those thighs
but give it a name though.
Maybe call it a bag of Skittles and just go taste the rainbow.
Butt smacks and hair pulling like I'm searching for tracks.
Yea, I want my baby to really feel how beautiful pain goes.
Let me penetrate those walls till your Niagara falls
and blissful serenity completes our union.
This is for all the women who still believe in fate,
Because whether Love is shown at first sight
Or grown in a fifth date,
The heart of all answers are found in your 'chess'
Where you can check your soul
before you find your mate.
Yea, I want to be your sweat.

But for now...

where cruel dreams can sometimes equal harsh realities.

You will remain an experience of the mind.

Till we meet again...

Taken

The chemistry was perfect.

Her beauty was unrivaled.

She was available

Yet he was taken.

Her phonebook filled with suitors

But her house was raided by looters.

Opportunists with angles.

Walls of happiness burned by recruiters

Who sold dreams of a home never meant for two

but drew intruders.

Social skills catfished by technology

Corrupt personalities peddled through computers.

Now, vulnerable was her property.

Insecurity littered her estate supplying ammunition,

Presenting easy targets for trained shooters.

Experience was a cruel teacher.

Her trust sensibilities failing to distinguish

the lesson from the tutor.

Those who dared scout her premises.

The lights were always on,

But no one was home.[11]

Because everyone was now guilty

The innocent were guilty by association.

Until she met him…

The timing was essential.

He wasn't interested in showing her the world.

Just her potential.

No need to highlight the subjects of her flaws.

Just a clear blackboard with no curriculum.

A blank slate with no agenda

Displaying the face of love

Without the show of a gender.

He was engaged in a relationship

Not even annoying habits presented reason or rhyme.

The only flaw involved was time.

The clock of routine.

Even its battery life was drained

by the doldrums of the day.

But she became an anomaly

In the dead space of his marriage.

For her, the carriage of burden lifts

During periods when thoughts of leaving his wife drifts.

Yet that wind always calms

Because his wife will always be in his loving arms.

Stolen are the jewels in these lands of signs

when a heist's at play.

Broke are the heavy hands of time.

But whenever he stares at his wife,

His clock of happiness will always be right twice a day.

To remind him of every compromise and sacrifice made.

Visions of her imperfect perfections cleared all fog.

And in the gravity of that space

The anomaly of her,

wanting so badly to be his other half.

She had no idea that she was in love

With a man she will never have.

The Cleft

There she lies

Like a cleft in a granite structure

Standing out when discovered

Well-secured when scrutinized

Solidified in the presence of lies.

There she resides

Embedded in the granite of our youth

Laying dormant throughout the ages

Until time exposes her truth.

Her building was fortified

Strengthened by manpower

Cemented with fear.

Her snipers with the itchy triggers

Laid in ambush...unaware.

For behold a storm was brewing

Planning its own danger.
Closing in from the north
advancing upon its unsuspecting stranger.

Thunderous signs provide notice
But ignorance is her influence
She tries to defend herself
under the torrent.
Except how does one shoot a storm?
Does a storm flinch in pain?
Does it bleed from affliction?
Sadly, some end up mistaking
their struggles...for addictions.

Yet she bleeds; the heart tears
Like a man walking upon sheet-rock.
And so her building crumbles;
falling just as fast as it was assembled.

Intelligent minds opened her doors

Curious eyes walked her floors

Old habits plundered her drawers

Greedy hands built her walls.

Her basement was a disarray

Cluttered with nowhere to move or hide.

That was until this storm

Found its way inside.

Can the truth be salvaged?

As we sift through the debris,

Let her be found

hidden in the depths of history.

Through a hole of old

will lay stories untold.

The crack that once

gave its structure an identity.

The cleft unchecked

Now became a chasm unrestrained.

Singes of the past

discolored the present.

These singes marked her victims;

the accidents that claimed innocence.

Singes from a small crevice

That widened under force.

Singes from the fissure

That broadened under pressure.

Except she is not burnt,

Nor has she drowned.

As a matter of fact,

She thrives on her lessons learned.

And there she survives.

She was oppressed, abused by false affections;

depressed at the mere sight of her reflection.

Until one day, she looked into the mirror

and suddenly smiled.

For God had looked back and whispered,

"my child".

Because she is beautiful, she is purity.

She endures all hardships.

Even the cleft that once threatened her security.

She is not seen in the art of the compliment

But in the seizing of the moment.

For she is that precious gift

Sent from God above

Who is she?

She is Love.

I Still See Love

I've seen love…

Face to face with hell's henchmen

To understand the ways by which they lynch men.

I've seen men stand behind pulpits and sermons

Preaching to love one another.

Yet they've crossed more heads than the Romans.

Mere hypocrites, too busy chasing women

Wasting time like cellphone calls on roaming;

And still only showing love

as nothing but an elusive omen.

I've seen love…

Love is being open to receive it;

The selflessness to pass it on.

She exposes cheap imitations,

Self-absorbed imaginations,

And inflated notions

Of what level she should be received on.

Love embraces those who seek its refuge

Like a shelter in the midst of a deluge.

Love explains the inexplicable

Simplifying the truth in due time;

She relays her message like a tactful pantomime.

Love heals the wounded in heart

Bringing closure to a past left open;

Because love with a lingering burden

Is like an overdue cast left unbroken.

I've seen love…

To love can mean provision for the best,

coming in the sacrifice for the worst.

To love is to thank God for showing us how He did it first.

To love can mean being left vulnerable

Where her words can cut sharper than knives;

Or can release hidden feelings

That set into motion the very discourse of our lives.

To love is mustering up enough to stay the course

Even when you know that timing may push that love

longer than your original intent.

But if her worth is shown in the waiting

Then her love must be patient.

To love is to remember when we first met

Because nowadays, even on clear nights,

I can only but catch your silhouette.

Grabbing love in glimpses

Why can't you just let me be?

Maybe because I still see love…

And one day she will find me.

Still, she behaved like a grieving widow

As if her last boyfriend was wearing a halo.

But to love, even under dimmed lights

Is the willingness to walk in her shadow.

For when the sun is due

And shines its brightness upon her…

So will it shine upon you.

Umbra

Standing like an inconspicuous prop against the wall,

I saw you.

Drained from the day's drudgery.

Finally relieved from duty,

Released from your eight hours of captivity.

The walls behind braced your fall

Like some trust building activity.

So I approached.

Picked you up.

You grabbed the hook handle

as I subtly pressed your bottom spring.

You encountered a few jokers in your past,

But this was more than just a Gotham thing.

I was under your influence.

Your distinct world became my clear reality.

Locked in my straightjacket of thoughts

Your asylum became my sanity.

My protection from the elements.

So just let your runner slide along my shaft

As I open up your nylon canopy.

Then the rain was felt,

The currents were fought.

Your storm drenched clothes and soaked thoughts.

But this was more than a sexual experience.

Because I remember those days in that darkest hour,

You were the shelter under the above torrent.

So I hid in your caves,

A fugitive arrested by love's warrant.

Tattered and torn

Withered and worn.

You rose to the occasion,

Held the fort,

Stood in the gap.

When my way was lost,

You were my X on the map.

Life was frozen in a desolate tundra,

But let the Romans salute you.

Because you are my “umbra”,

My parasol, my shade, my shelter.

You are the rib in the canopy of my umbrella.

Where dreams never fold with the wind,

Nor break against it.

VI. Lost & Found

Empty Bottles and Ashtrays

They stood on windowsills and refrigerator tops

…like trophies.

Encased in glass,

These bronze medals replaced gold remnants

of a childhood past.

Competition was a visceral stimulant.

It fueled those glory days.

A true phase;

the aide came from the culmination of talent and effort,

swayed by adulation and praise.

Rewards for dues paid.

Nothing but empty bottles and flasks…

Filled to its brim,

with flashes of nights gone too fast.

Just to mask memories of a child

Watching his mother using her last breaths

To heave food that couldn't stay down.

Glimpses of bedridden days,

Where her only smile was featured

when I entered the room…unannounced.

Then being swiftly whisked away by my father.

Shot glasses became ashtrays;

the inhale of smoke to fill the lungs and replace the pain.

A void of album pictures,

Most of which I can't remember.

Memories exacerbated by headaches of the morning after.

Ashes of "when is mommy coming home?"

And "why did she leave?"

Littered my clean streets,

Paved by salted streaks

falling from reddened cheeks.

Wondering why did God take her away?

Or maybe it was the schoolyard fights.

The bloodstained clothes of an adolescent

who wore pain on sleeves.

…God didn't have angels, he sent thieves…

Then shed this guilt with autumn leaves.

But allow me to grieve

through the trophies of my proclivities.

Because in the dawn of sober minds,

These empty bottles and ashtrays can never replace time.

It can never replenish this brain with new memories.

All that remains is an ingrained photograph

of a fat baby in a tub, cuddled in his mother's arms.

Yearning to clutch her one more time.

Hessa

She made me nervous.

Thoughts of failure acquiesced

to the beauty of her presence.

Because she was the moment,

and anyone who seized her…

…Captured greatness.

Every time I envisioned her face

My heart skipped a beat.

Yet the preparation before the approach

was always the toughest.

I used to believe I was bright

Until thoughts of her superseded what I wanted to recite.

Sweaty palms and momentary lapses

into alternate endings or a parallel universe,

Blank stares into the daytime oblivion.

Dreams of the confident debonair

Sweeping her off weak knees

with calculated words so enticing.

Visions were inviting like Sunday dinner to my writing.

I always wished I were him.

That man with his virtual pedigree

who could do no wrong in parallel worlds.

Or maybe those pearls were locked deep in the mind.

Jewels bolted by doubt, fear and perception.

But since inception,

I've faced many mirrors,

where life needed to be spoken into my reflection.

And in the understanding of who you are,

Not caring about your reception.

The night was here and I saw her.

I remembered bumping into her by accident

and feeling the helpless loss of control.

But knowing with certainty that this was where I belonged.

I heard her.

I felt her returning her gaze.

What to say…what to do??

Words fought with multiple thoughts.

Sentences became fragmented

Bones of phrases memorized

Return to memory disjointed.

Dreams about to meet reality in the making;

Pronouns shaking

Focus breaking

Verbs and adjectives become scrambled with bacon…

Damn, why am I talking about bacon.

Maybe I need to eat, no I just ate.

But I need to feel complete,

Back out now or just meet fate.

Maybe just one more drink to settle the mind

to link experiences with age.

Wisdom freed from its cage.

Let thoughts flow to her as if being read off the page.

But I'm not ready.

What if…

And then she calls my name…

"and next to the stage…"

The curtains roll back

I've been here before.

Showtime…

Listen

A young man approached me and asked,
"Press, let me hear you spit something".
To which I said, "Close your eyes".
And I began…
To listen means to hear with intention.
Listen, I want to hear a message
that reaches ears around town.
I want to hear your faith flow fluently
with a flair that flings fears
and chills hairs, echoing on surround sound.
I want to hear your persuasive diction
that gives me a light bulb type addiction
to persevere myself off the ground.
I want to hear your cutting-edge inspiration
With a little bit of spice for when I feel down.
So that when I return the favor,

I can speak that word onto your tongue
With a little bit of flavor you can savor.
I want to inhale gentle verbs
And let it stimulate my mind like a mental herb.
For example, what does it mean to love,
to captivate, to take?
Premise: I *love* her…why?
Because she is the helium in my balloon of euphoria
Whose smile propels my existence thru joyless clouds
Into a thin atmosphere where she *captivates* my lungs,
and *takes* my breath away.

I want to feel some of those punch lines
That makes you want to throw in the towel.
I want to figure out some of those Wheel of Fortune type
Phrases that make you want to buy a vowel.
I want to hear your tailor-made storylines
and not your stolen trends.

Because in the end,

I want to free-dive in metaphors so deep,

I catch the Bends.

I want to hear bars

Of imagery that gives hope for the seasons.

I want to hear alliteration from young stars

Searching for truth and something to believe in

So that when they find both,

I can sit back and watch

Real rappers rhythmically wrapping riddles around reason.

I want to hear rhyme schemes that outline themes

And not just your vocabulary skills

sounding like a crime scene.

You know, unconnecting "hit-and-run" type thoughts

Leaving witnesses at the scene traumatized

and in total confusion.

Where your audience tries to comprehend

What you just said and they receive a contusion.
Because they say the brain only retains
10% of what is spoken
which would make what you just said to me an allusion.
So take a step back and just listen to yourself.
Understand who you are, and like the old adage goes…
"to thine ownself be true".[12]

Sometimes I get speechless
when I listen to those pleas of Polonius.
So then give me that unspoken word;
give me some Bach, Beethoven, Wynton,
Dizzy, Coltrane, Duke, Louis, Jelly Roll, Charlie P, Fats,
and who can play those sweet keys like Thelonius.

Then what would I want to hear from myself
when I grace your stage?
I want to hear clips of my thoughts

Load thru these lips like a Smith & Wesson;

So when I cock, pull that trigger and explode,

You can feel my life's trips, but for all its gifts & blessings.

I want to hear my cohesive ideas, sticking to the point

Like an adhesive that coats my faith with acrylic.

Knowing that any doubts in a God

who has brought me out of despair,

would just make the bones of my message arthritic.

So here I flow to you in a zone,

In a place where peace is now my home;

And now I can stand in the face of any critic…

because I've already faced my own.

I told the young man to open his eyes and I said,

"To listen means to hear with intention...

...did you listen?

Or do you still want to hear something??"

VII. Arise

Flies

They swarm around ripe produce when least expected.
All it takes is one delayed night
Not tossing out the trash you keep.
They creep undetected silently in the air
smelling your harbored waste as you sleep.
But you reap what you sow,
The blow of time when you react slow.
Then you awaken to the kitchen stench.
Lazy is the mood
Until you see the full-fledged fruit-fly infestation
feeding off fermented food.
Ever tried getting rid of these bastards quickly??
Not happening.

Built to find you fast through cracked windows.

Their sense of smell goes where the wind blows.

These tiny burglars would be caught easily with legs made.

Others hitch rides from your grocery stores with eggs laid.

You see, when you finish tasks late.

Your problems can reproduce at fast rates.

Yet even when complacency was your weakness,

Let patience be your last bait.

Gallant is fruitless efforts

Of near success tasted.

Then they multiply.

Waiting too long brings the cause & effect

Of a talent wasted.

In the midst of defeat,

My grandmother would lure their noses to a treat.

Give your unwanted villager

something sweet before you snap.

Patience and a little apple cider vinegar,

complete for your trap.

L.O.E. (Live Or Exist)

Oscar Wilde once said,

"To live is the rarest thing in the world,

Most people exist…that is all".[13]

Meandering misfits moving mindlessly

through mazes of mediocrity.

Going through phases of feelings,

In daydreams, subconscious gazes.

The cyclical motions

souls in restless oceans.

Old habits on an elliptical past

Bold rabbits running,

going nowhere fast.

But this city was not built for the weak.

Harboring heavy sandbags of walls

battle-tested and ready.

Steady in form

So when storms came,

They transformed into levies.

Weary is the heart & body,

Emotional sentinels

Guarding unlit posts at all times.

Nine to six becomes 6'9,

As work becomes a tall grind.

Or maybe we are just a big world of thoughts,

living in cities of small minds.

Stubborn as an ox, but I'm a fox

when I think outside this box.

This world holding keys to living life's fullest moments.

Unlock those rusted windows

And allow that brisk invigorating air into your home.

Because this key to life is found only

by embracing the fear of the unknown.

And in there, in that miniscule attic

As the heart is weighed on the scale of faith,

grounded on planted feet.

Is where future Kings and Queens

shall sit, heirs to the throne.

And the question shall be asked,

Are you living…or simply existing??

Surge

Rise from the ashes O' restful soul.
Be consumed by the spirit of the awoken Phoenix.
Though adversity has ruptured damaged coils
Let resilience repair the springs in your broken helix.
When sleep is your only comfort,
The nightmares vivid through opened eyes.
How can we feel the sun at its brightest,
Veiled through cloakened skies?
Lost in a circle of thoughts
the rain of doubt shown.
Stuck in a familiar town
You know you've already outgrown.

But stay the course my friend
Even when it seems the wilderness has no end.
Visualize the forest from the trees

that camouflage your blessings around the bend.
Extend those arms in your darkness
And you shall find the ones who pretend.
The ones on whose shoulders you sought to depend
And were nowhere to be found.
You looked to the East for help to share burdens
stacked on your back by the pounds.
Expect no handouts in this life.
When phone calls are made,
And the crickets laugh at your sounds.
When the problems build
with the waves of tomorrow ready to overwhelm.
Be steady and know
that you are still Captain at the helm.
Feel the internal compass between sinew and bone.
Identify your direction for destinations unknown.
Fret not on the time to come,
For today has enough problems of its own.

Whether triumphant or tragic,

Leave nothing to happenstance.

Let your will to overcome,

Be bigger than your circumstance.

Now arise….

Though the journey has been draining and tough

You have rested long enough.

We have work to do.

VIII. Footprints of Destiny

The Prodigal Son

Spend it so lavishly.

Gifts seized so savagely.

Taken for granted until it's forsaken.

Voids left vacant.

Filled by the sucker punch from the butt of a gun

From which he never awakened.

Life spiraling out of control,

The cracks of identity started breaking.

Teetering on the brink,

Resting on the rocks.

But let him drink this bond

between knowing self and situation,

Where it's stirred but never shaken.

Invincible was the thought.

As family, he believed that words should be brought.

And if resolution could not be sought,

Let the last resort be in his mind

"at least we fought".

In the struggle to find meaning,

Here is where the search stays.

Replays of staring down the barrel of a weapon cocked

He wanted to hit his foe in the worst way.

The insult of intimidation

Knowing this kid a decade plus,

Going back to those church days.

"Just put that gun down and lets even up this fight".

But it wasn't to be.

It was in the months that followed

Where the insult of the incident turned to disappointment.

The pride of revenge turned to sadness.

The madness of a night that could've been avoided.

In hindsight, he realized his tongue was double edged.

Able to bless and curse with precision.

He spoke his blunt realities

Of someone who took advantage of relationships.

An altercation that quickly shifted outdoors.

But no matter how frustrating,

More words should've been spoken privately.

The tongue should've been used to encourage and edify.

The blame can easily be spread,

Yet what do we tell our youth?

We fall apart when emotions enter bloodstreams

Leaving the heart to fill up the head.

When situations needed to simmer,

Maybe our best weapon is not in our hands nor guns,

But in holding up our mirrors.

His gifts created a rift that went adrift.

Soon, even musical instruments sent in a prior life

Were used to pay rent and other habits.

But when you fail to squeeze your talents

through opened windows,

Adversity can grab it.

And suddenly all of his talents vanished…

His resources disappeared,

Dried in a desert's sun.

Savoring in the satisfaction of self-indulgence.

The relish of relaxation rejoicing in recreation.

The glee of gratification,

Guiding the gross negligence of gifts.

Living in the luxury of life's leisure.

Testing the thrills of time wasting.

Delighting in the diversions of doing nothing.

Focused on the family film featuring a father's failures.

Only to understand that there was always One,

Eternal in his love.

With open arms still extended…

For the prodigal son.

Why I Do This?

Because the knife wouldn't budge in midair…

A machete's momentum manipulated by memories.

His tendencies were deconstructive,

Negative criticisms mixed with cynicism.

Always being told what you can't do,

Should've done, or should be.

Was controlled by the belt

And whatever was felt by his mood swings.

But when this dude swings,

Blood and tough skin mingles with the dribble of the lips,

So out pours rude things.

The mouth can be a superb lid.

But the heart spoke truth,

Festering like bacteria under the tongue

Was where his verbs hid.

Why I do this?

Because even though he was a light sleeper,

Learned over time,

All it took was knowing every creek

in those hardwood floors.

Movements always done on the inhale.

But those snores on the exhale were the indicator.

I saw a mercenary, an evil twin

trying to fulfill his duties as the hired might.

Propelled by flashes of losing battles in wired fights.

But on this day even light sleepers have tired nights.

And on the inhale,

One downward plunge will end his burden

Of being both mother and father,

and my misery of being the worse son ever.

Ready to give up

because I could never live up to his standards.

Why I do this?

Because it took me fifteen years later,

to finally release that knife.

In-between that life was the loyalty of a fool;

I was too busy stabbing myself.

Searching for validation of my existence through him;

Skim through the slim survival

of black males in hoods with futures grim.

Sutures and skin

couldn't close constant cuts of kin.

Drowning in pools of perilous predicaments

filled to the brim.

To think with the extended limbs of wisdom

Is where we learn to either sink or swim.

Because of him, I lost everything.

Because of him, I found myself.

Why I do this?

I do this for the voiceless.

To illustrate love

to anyone who has ever slept in a cell or a train.

To articulate hope

to those who make their homes on pavements,

in cardboard boxes and shelters.

To authorize faith in the midst of failure.

I do this for the forgotten.

Fatherless communities riddled with drugs and bullets.

Our race ignored and incarcerated.

Suppressed with prejudice,

killed by fear until we become a lost breed.

While others are dispersed;

Neighborhoods gentrified by the cost of greed.

Its job creation, that's how they sell it.

I do this because a friend once said

If you say nothing, someone else will…

But don't be mad at how they tell it.

Why I do this?

Because when situations looked grim,

I found another way to fight.

The District Attorney was faxed my defense and told the

detective that the description of charges

Didn't match what he typically read from a defendant….

…because this kid can write.

Funny, what I strayed away from ended up saving my life.

Now I do this for the jail cells crowded with floaters.

Non violent drug offenders and young men as numbers

fulfilling the pressures of a cop's end of the month quotas.

While some states get to legalize, tax and profit

Off the very same drugs young minorities

have been incarcerated for.

The systemic and institutional racism

From discriminatory traffic stops and fines

That increase state budgets to the killings of unarmed men.

To the schools that do poorly at standardized testing,

Because the companies that create our most important state

and national exams also publish our textbooks;

which low income districts can't afford.[14]

Sometimes we can centralize our anger on one phase.

But we can't blame the trap that kills the mouse,

if we don't understand who built the maze.

To understand that the pages of our history

are filled with more than just slaves.

Before Columbus 'discovered' these shores;

Before Eriksson and his Vikings,

There were the Phoenicians and their oars.

Confirmed by Native Americans,

"Black skinned people had come from the south east

in boats, trading in gold-tipped spears"[15].

So even from the journals of Columbus himself we ignore.

Before we were poor,

Before the Europeans had libraries,

In Spain there were the Moors.

Before the Incas, Mayans, and Aztecs,

There were the Olmecs.

Before the Rothchilds, Rockefellers, & Fords,

There was the Malian Emperor Mansa Musa;

the wealthiest of them all.

I do this because no matter your color or creed,

Historical ignorance will always leave you susceptible

to repeating familiar mistakes.

Why I do this?

Because my mother died of rheumatic fever

when I was three.

Rumors said she was killed by a heavy heart,

And back then I thought it was me.

Now I look back on my life with my father,

And all the women mistreated with illusive futures to be.

For every time a hit was taken by me.

For every moment he's said

"son, you resemble your mother",

I knew she was free.

The Jump

I sat at 13,000 feet watching the panorama below.

The show of confidence mangled

While legs dangled with death.

My breath was short,

As the thought to jump held criminal court

with fear and other emotional sorts.

They fought the brief defense of logic.

I sat on the precipice

staring into the abstract abyss of the unknown.

But on the word go, I had to let go.

Let go of all doubts, insecurities, and failures.

To face this fear

that paralyzed movements into stagnancy for so long.

Now I was truly doing what I wanted to do.

Before I was busy building other people's dreams,

Taking up residence in futures not my own.

So embrace this sweet death.

Because in the chase for perfection,

I'd never felt more alive than in this race.

Humbled in this rapid decent through gravity's space.

So taste these clouds.

The rush of the freefall, the cold winds

Fighting to send the body back up.

The atmospheric pressure grew as dots in the earth

became recognizable houses and familiar landmarks.

Fog in the goggles blurred vision and horizon's line.

Time seemed forever as up became down,

And the ground opened its canvas quickly.

An uncontrollable rollercoaster with no seats to clutch,

as if that would somehow cushion my fall.

Then came the sudden jerk of the parachute,

opening its arms into the expanse of the sky.

As the elements gathered like Titans,

breathing envelopes of gust

into my ballooned contraption.

They cradled my speed

until I became one with the wind.

I left the plane lifeless.

Quarantined with the bold

airborne like a virus.

The pollen of mediocrity infected the nose

Then put pressure on my iris.

I couldn't see, think, nor breathe correctly,

as the headache of adversity gave my brain a sinus.

Now my dreams had wings.

I sat on that ninth cloud above basking in glory

Beneath my feet were the evergreens and cypress.

So let this adrenaline become contagious,

Because I was put here to spread this itch of freedom

until it becomes a crisis.

You can't capture God's beauty

from your best penthouse roof.

My eyes were opened through the wilderness.

Taken from sleeping on floors sightless,

To not having a clue that my view from the top

would ever be this…priceless.

Epilogue

Thank You

For the ones who weren't there when I wanted them.

But God-sent when I needed them.

Sent through different seasons for different reasons,

Frostbitten by one on those days freezing.

Believing that he was my only bloodline

To the affirmation of who I was.

Then I crossed paths with a family of few,

Who became the glue in the lost shoe of hospitality.

To the ones who invested in the forced dues of reality.

In the apartment below the Jodhan family slept

And went through those nights of frustration we wept.

A tenant who became a big sister.

Roxanne, in those times where giving up seemed imminent,

you were a temporary buffer

of impeccable wisdom through the hardships.

May those young boys be blessed

And know that all is possible

When you can put your mind to it.

To the one who's bright charm

Glowed and showed in a hood

Where there was never a night's calm.

We always fought each other

as kids on the basketball courts,

But in war he is my right arm.

Regarded by him as the thinker.

To be able to think my way out during the storms & clouds.

He had taken a step back to see me step forward.

And I hope he will be proud.

To his brother…Ace.

I remember those days with cabinets bare

It was rare to see no agendas behind his ability to share.

Makes sense when you see their mother's care.

When all wasn't at its best,

All I possessed was a suitcase,

You supplied clothes and a place to rest.

Wherever there is death's harm,

You'll always be my left arm.

And to the one who became my heart.

She took on the family scars with me.

Those weary nights she stayed up

And slept in the car with me.

She presented ears to listen.

Rebooted the hard drive

Then reinstalled hope in my system.

Even her friends to whom I'm indebted,

Took in a stranger on the strength of her.

Allegiance was the Achilles heel.

Hit by arrows of bad choices

That ripped through skin and the marrow's shield.

But they say "an expert is a man who has made

All the mistakes which can be made, in a narrow field".[16]

And there you will find these pages.

Failures fit in flawed folders.

Let those memories of the selfless,

And to whom much is given and required.

Be laid on these broad shoulders.

Footnotes:

1. John Ray's collection of English proverbs (1670, 1678)
2. 1994 December 14, Usenet discussion message, Newsgroup: alt.buddha.short.fat.guy, From: Ernst Berg at moamiex.com, Subject: Thinking Out Loud. (Google Groups Search)
3. Desiderius Erasmus, http://www.brainyquote.com/quotes/quotes/d/desiderius161329.html
4. John Locke, Some Thoughts Concerning Education, 1692
5. Proverbs 22:15 (KJV)
6. Samuel Butler, Hudibras, Part II (1664)
7. Proverbs 29:15 (KJV)
8. www.mortonsalt.com/our-history/history-of-the-morton-salt-girl

9. www.visionaryeyecare.wordpress.com/2008/08/04/eye-test-find-your-blind-spot-in-each-eye/
10. www.globalresearch.ca/the-prison-industry-in-the-united-states-big-business-or-a-new-form-of-slavery/8289
11. When the Lights Are On But Nobody's Home: A Book That Brings Reality Back To Make You Think… Again by Phyllis Zuccarello (2012)
12. William Shakespeare, Hamlet Act 1, Scene 3, 78.
13. Oscar Wilde, The Soul of Man under Socialism, 1891
14. http://www.theatlantic.com/features/archive/2014/07/why-poor-schools-cant-win-at-standardized-testing/374287/
15. http://www.globalresearch.ca/before-columbus-how-africans-brought-civilization-to-america/5407584
16. Niels Henrik David Bohr (1885-1962), Nobel Prize for Physics in 1922.

www.ingramcontent.com/pod-product-compliance
Lightning Source LLC
LaVergne TN
LVHW051644080426
835511LV00016B/2492
9780692378786